– HOW –
TO HOST
A DEMON

HOW TO HOST A DEMON

CAITLIN JACKSON

atmosphere press

This book is dedicated to all the ghosts
—past, present and future—
that I'm lucky enough to encounter in recovery.

Table of Contents

Section I: Shadow Mapping

Section II: Anatomy of a Nightmare

Section III: Screaming in my Day Dreams

"We cross our bridges when we come to them and burn them behind us, with nothing to show for our progress except a memory of the smell of smoke, and a presumption that once our eyes watered."

– Tom Stoppard

Section I

—

Shadow Mapping

Dreamscapes

I.

Before I fall asleep

there is a horse
delicate, despite his size.

Gasp,
something triggers the thought
and then a vivid movie memory—
denim friction.

Desperate—I thought
I had found my fairytale. A prince,
too Teflon handsome:
I slid right off when he reached for me.

II.
In this one,
I am driving myself to the airport.

I often do not make it to my destination.

Sometimes I find the nearest gas station
and stare for a long time at the fountain drinks,
pretending to consider the Dr. Pepper
before going to the cans
so bright in the corner of my eye.

As the dream ends,
I will slam the car door
and snap each one open
with a satisfying hiss and raise...

III.

In Paris, our cab is forever crashing into things and I am forever
trying to pronounce my dinner order, an endless string of words
that probably mean either *sauce* or *chicken.*
Strangers are always laughing at my mouth
and stupid tongue.

I get away to look for gargoyles,

or sometimes it is to buy a crêpe.

Sometimes, but not often, it is to see the cathedral,
the one with impossible stained-glass windows like something from
    a dream
while I'm dreaming. Space folding over
onto itself.

Sometimes I am there and so is a boy
who puts his hand over mine.

Sometimes we are swept up in a war beyond our comprehension,
pursued by a mysterious and deadly enemy,

or sometimes all the glass shatters and I hear a scream from far off,

then closer and closer.

I am climbing the stairs to the top of Notre Dame. They go on
    forever
and I am so hot and sweaty in my ski jacket, breathing hard until
    finally I find the gargoyle at home
in his archway. He's been there all along, crouched and waiting
    with hollow eyes.

IV.
There are bottles all around my room.
They are under my bed.

They are in my cupboards
and the suitcases I'm packing.

I keep finding them, but I can't
seem to raise them to my lips.

They are rolling away from me
across the floor.

And often I am trying to call you

with pebbles at your window,
howling silent in the night.

I keep packing and bottles keep appearing
and sometimes someone is coming and I have to hide them.

Sometimes they are taken from me
and thrown away.

But always am I alone when I find them,
chiming around my feet,
tolling like bells.

V.
I have to remember to thank you
for the diet cherry Coke
that's cold, already in the fridge at midnight
when we come home.

And thank you for the blue of our walls with the green
of your eyes. I'm burning bright red
surrounded by cool ocean colors.

I have made it home safe
and coherent and we will all just
leave it at that for now, I think, won't we?
Let's wait to see where this future is headed;
we all know it's a long fall from here.

We've made it before, but another—
maybe not so lucky.

I am so thirsty today.
10am and already on my fourth glass
of water. At least.

How much is luck, how much
is *I just wasn't quite ready*
to explode? Not just yet?

I am blinking this morning.
Fifth glass of water.

Last night I had no dreams at all.

Cat and Mouse

An addict's word means nothing
without action.
I would argue it means nothing
with it either, the action itself
carrying little currency
from one hour to the next
as your mind ticks around the clock,
reason scurrying like mice
in a fable where a hungry cat
tricks them, one after another,
into his waiting mouth.

How to explain that though
you see the jagged teeth,
all the mind registers
just before jaw snaps shut
is a friendly smile?

More important, still:
the mouse, half-blind,
has nowhere else to go.

Convenience

Why am I always dreaming
that I'm walking into gas stations?
I can hear the tinny doorbell
sound over and over as I go in
and out again then in—
an alarm that someone is here
for their fix.

I'm scanning the wine shelf,
searching the coolers for
spiked seltzer.

Last time I was drinking
I drove to the 711 and bought some hard
strawberry lemonade.
At first I couldn't—
it was before 7am.
So I sat in the car with
my eyes shut and music on,
looking over my shoulder in the still
dark parking lot.
Until a half hour ticked by
and when I went back,
the cashier looked at me with such sad eyes.
Better that than
the rolling eyes of so many doctors.
You're lucky to be alive.
An attack and scolding
in the name of helping.

Fuck you
I told the nurse, fluids leaking
into my weak veins.

It is not luck
I have been working hard
to keep the liquor
down only in my dreams.

I'm not proud of any of this—
not the losses
and certainly not the wins.

I'm so tired of keeping score each minute of every day and night.

Once I woke with a black eye.
I had to sit, ashamed, in a circle—
a whipping boy like in a book I read
in third grade.
It wasn't fair then.
it isn't fair now.

That's life, right?

But aren't you supposed to fight
to change it?
It will never be a perfect sphere,
but at least polish
it until it glows.

Instead, I opted out
with big gulps of liquor
for every laugh I heard
at my expense.
I can still hear the chuckles pour
like gin.

And after the glass door chimes, I'm watching
a woman sweeping up pieces of a doughnut,
and I'm not sure if this is a dream
or a memory,
if I am drunk
or sober,
if I drove here
or walked,
and she looks at me and sighs.

I put three boxes of wine on the counter and hand her my card.
She stares a moment at my shaking hand
then rolls her eyes.

Strong Swimmer

I look at pictures
of your life online.
I'm in a fight
that feels one-sided,
and still I'm losing somehow.
Sobriety can go so fast—
just one white knuckle hour and you're out—
back to the worst you ever were.

And I haven't said your name out loud,
not really,
for years.
Remember when
you whispered *King Lear*
into my ear?
There was a tragedy building
off the coast of our story.

The storm clouds can roll in so fast
and lightning always scared me.
It should, I think.

He doesn't think so,
never jumps at the shrieking ghost.
Never screams or startles.

Not like you—big green eyes
so filled with fear.
But you were more human, maybe.
More ready to admit
the ways you were weak.

I used to fall asleep holding my phone
for both of you.
Please wait, we appreciate
your patience,
your understanding.

My life has been one elevator song
after another. I wait but there's never
a click on the line.
And the symphony is shrunk down
and chewed up over our bad connection.
Remember back when we had wires
tying us together?

My life is wasting
waiting by phone after phone.
And now I write my poems
on a pallid glowing screen
and forget what I learned back then,
back when you were mine.

And I dream again and again
everyone I love always leaves me.
But you...
you just stopped loving me
then stuck around.
That was worse.
And I know it's a matter of time
before he will too.

I pretended to be drowning,
but my stroke is strong
and the ocean makes me fierce.

I lied to him—
said I was weak.
But in the end they all find out
when I make it to the beach—
standing on the sand, dripping
heavy and embarrassed.

The Hitching Post

The old bar will be waiting for me
indefinitely.
It has stood there longer than I've been alive
and probably will continue forever—
the building equivalent
of a cockroach in nuclear winter.

It will be waiting
for me to throw back four more gin
and tonics with such relief,
I made even the grizzled bartender flinch.

I was never sturdy.
I always cried too easily.

I don't stop driving today,
but I turn to clock it anyway:
the dirty building, circled
by a herd of lurking pickups.
Just you wait, I say. Maybe I'll
be back for you,
I don't know,
it's not safe to make promises.
But I can say
it won't be today.

And yet. Still.

There's something about giving in
that makes it the most pleasing of all seductions,
something about just *"fuck it"*
that you can hold in your hand
like a dying butterfly
flapping tissue wings
as hard as it can.
It might never rise again,
but it can dream still of flight—
so clear for a moment
it's nearly real.

Relapse

The living room smells like vomit now.
It's no wonder—
I threw up here on the couch
two days ago.
You said I could have died choking, but
I could only laugh.
So many nights I was left alone
with not even a word
but a bottle always there for me,
sitting in the same sticky spot.
A path from couch to counter
nearly worn into our tile floor
from my sliding feet,
the same floor I rolled over
and threw up on Wednesday at 2am.
Mostly sober for three years and
now I'm someone who can't hold my liquor.

It used to be my only charming trait.

And were you just upset because
if I had died,
I would have won....?

'Til death do us part, after all.

Clockwork Dreams

It's true I loved you fast;
maybe there was a scheme,
or was it just a dream?
Guess it depends who's baiting
the hook. And who
the worm is today. Feminine wiles
are something you learned to distrust
before you could even walk.

Most people's dreams fade
as they go through their mornings.
Mine haunt me every hour on the hour,
a timepiece that never fails—
and don't you like to repair clockwork?

This vision had its teeth in me deep.
Made me plot like a witch,
collecting newt eyes,
stirring her cauldron below grasping
black branches.
I'll curse you to hell
or turn you into a toad.

Or I'll love you with a love that's true.

That's rich.
Audacious was never me—
I was mumbling spells
beneath my breath
a long time before I met you.

All I have now, though:
just patience and tears
and lots of wishes
on the last bites of pies
and dandelion fluff.

We're scattered to the winds now, aren't we?

But still, when you look at me,
you just see turning gears,
grinding mashing
everything in my path into dust.
It turns out
you don't know me at all—
not one piece of me is machinery.

I fooled myself

after all,
you've never been on your knees,
but I used to pray every night.
Can you even bend that way?

I got a stand mixer for Christmas.
It's light blue
and I'll make you brownies
for your birthday.
Happy birthday to you
and Jesus Christ.
Except the stars say somehow
it was not even his birthday on the 25th;
instead it was just when the wise men
arrived to see him toddle
through the hay to stroke
a curious donkey's velvet muzzle.

I wish I could give you gold—
myrrh and frankincense
would just make you sneeze.

I am so tired
and I cannot take a picture
of my fingers splayed to share
with the world
and say *finally.*
Knife into bone,
I carved our initials
in the back of my skull.
But you only write
in pencil.

Erase me
limb by limb
on Christmas morning.

Runaway

I soaked up the cold sunset,
tried to burn my image
into the eastern horizon.
This far north, the darkness is a comfort.
I love the woods with you.
Can we go for a walk,
start something new?
I've been thinking lately
with my foot out the door,
but I can never bring myself to take my leave.

I have the taste of regret burned into eyeballs—
synesthesia without the hallucinogens.
I'm always scared I will evolve to be
schizophrenic,
delusions lying in wait like hungry jungle cats.
And maybe it's just a crazy vision:
me finally
closing the door behind,
shaking at the stoplight,

the tremendous decision
of whether to let it pass my lips
swinging over my neck.

Rust

I'm always trying to find Mars with the naked eye.
I'm burning up in the sun
of my own fury at being
cut loose at my own ends.
You always are building walls up
and then promptly crunching
through my defenses.
The only sanctuary I have is outer space.
It's cold out there
and you can't see the stars for the galaxy.
I want to get as far
out as possible
until there's no light, only dark matter
going straight to my head.

I'm delirious by the middle of the night.
The gin used to keep me up
until 2am,
big mouthfuls
just to make the stupor last.

I can't help picking fights
when my orbit is Jupiter aligned.
Saturn has all the rings.
I'm so jealous.
Neptune has all the seas.
I'll swim through them when I'm dead at last.
Let's take a tour of the planets
on donkey back,
down into the cold depths

where eyeballs freeze and pop.
Solace finally
with my blood frozen solid
and nothing of the Earth left
to tarnish my skin.

Seashore Convalescence

I am walking through dune after dune,
trying to get to the ocean
that keeps slipping away
into the horizon,
where city lights dance
full of revelers
that I'll never meet.

Sometimes it's night or sometimes
it's just before, the sun
setting over darkening waters.

And somehow I'm always ending up
at the soccer fields where I watched
my brother play.

Now it's your daughter—
she's keeping goal.
I'm drinking in the car.
In my dreams the thermos is always green
and I shed tiny liquor bottles
like scales off my silvery skin.

For abruptly I am a fish
stuck in the dunes,
the sands suffocating.
Always waiting for you
to pick me up by the tail
and toss me back.

Parking Lot Rituals

I've tried to turn into
a witch.
I mumble incantations,
shuffle decks of tarot cards,
grow black flowers
in our front yard.

Did I ensorcell you?
Pick my teeth with rodent bones
and wave my hand
above your beer glass...
A brainwashing potion.

If I could control your mind,
I would have made you fall in love
with someone much more sane.
Maybe that nice girl
your friend brought to the bar
that one night near Christmas.
I doubt you even knew.
You drank four tulip glasses
of something called Hairy Eyeball
and fell asleep in the parking lot.

I drove home and got
a bacon egg and cheese sandwich for dinner.
I watched an old man
feed two golden retrievers ice cream cones
in the bed of his pickup,
their soft pink tongues
lapping the vanilla swirl
melting down his wrinkled hands.

As I put on my blinker
to make the right turn home,
one let out a short, sharp bark.

Seven miles away, you curled up
in your cold front seat,
as gone as I would be for years.
I cast spell after spell
to exorcise us
and sometimes still in the night,
I wake up thinking
I've heard that sharp bark
splitting the air.

Floating Castles

Clouds outside my left elbow.

I slept on the airplane
and dreamt we fell out of the sky
over and over again.
Panicked, I grabbed your knee
and willed myself back to sleep,
even with the plunge of the drop
still lurching in my stomach.
It's nothing new.

We're plummeting and on fire
in my nightmares all the time.
I slept in a tent
as the world ended
and searched for you to no avail.
Finally, when the oceans rose,
I stepped in and found you.

I've jumped out of an airplane, but you never did.

I was just going along
for the ride,
but didn't realize you couldn't get off
after you leapt through the door.
Life is like that, but they don't ask
if you want to go,
just push you out.

Down we go again. I'm gasping
but you can't hear it above the engine noise.
I don't want to shatter

into a million pieces,
lost in flames. I look out and see fields—
land below.
This is no good.

I want my bones to rest at sea.

Orlando International Airport

The second we touch down, heartburn flares into my throat—
a volcano channeling the weather outside.
I'm pining
and enraged to walk into the heat again.

I thought maybe for a second—
with the wet leaves,
black branches cold rain baptizing as we held hands
at the pinnacle of our hike
and we took deep breaths.
I thought about leaping.

I don't live here a lady clutching
a GQ tote screams into her phone.
And you turn and say *This is a hot mess.*

And I am,
I am so tired.
I should always have a smile for you—
that was the deal, wasn't it?
And no one has ever seen me cry over you.
Not even my oldest friends,
but tears still fall silent in a forest
or an airport when no one's looking.
I *do* live here,
But this is not my home.

There's a lump in my throat
and the exhaust fumes
in the humid air
are making me sick.

I dreamt the whole way down here
that my lungs were filled with icy fluid
and I couldn't even scream.

It was heaven.

Section II

—

Anatomy of a Nightmare

Playing Games

You ask what I want from you.
I remember seventeen, whispering
under covers, fingers
barely touching, my head pressed
to hear heartbeat percussion.

We used to play a game:
when did you first love me?
What do you think of
when you hear me laugh—?
A breath of cold clean air.

I know you're not one
for being sentimental,
and I'm both leftovers
and a fur-laden trapper lying in wait,
teeth bared in the dark,
head cocked listening for
the sharp crack of bone.
You couldn't limp away from me
if you tried.

And I remember, oh,
instead of monster—
eyes glowing red—
when I was fresh air
and soft fingertips. But
tonight I crawl back beneath the bed
I don't belong in.

Those days have passed.
Now I rip flesh from sinew
and laugh in the dark.

Easy Virtue

Pink satin bow
lost in the grass.
My dog deems it
barely worth a sniff
as we walk by,
but my eyes linger.

A quick transition and I'm no longer
strolling through these woods but
I'm slamming a car door
outside a bookstore
on a strange campus in Atlanta.
You told me to whisper
so your mom wouldn't hear me on the phone.
Then we walked inside, inhaled deep,
and you bought me what would become
one of my favorite books.

Six years later you were long, long gone
and I watched the movie version,
plastered on my parent's couch.
Too drunk to see those water-blue eyes.

And there are children on the nearby playground.
It is possible I know their mom.
Maybe we went to high school together
and played manhunt with you.

The bow is covered in mud and we step over it.
It isn't for us in this life.
And the children's voices follow me home.

If I cry, it's my fault.

I wonder what ours
would have said.

Himself

After dreaming some mornings
it feels like I'm so close I could
turn my head and continue a long-ago-
dropped conversation,
picked up as though the years
hadn't happened and I just dismounted
From my horse worried for a test tomorrow—
an essay my GPA. The only numbers
I ever cared about
were the ones I thought would let me escape.

If you have a certain look, they tell you
these are the best years of your life.
No one ever said that to me.
Wait until you're out of your twenties
they said instead.

Then I was dead by 34,
never good at waiting.
Brought back to life by visions of him
and you
and horses.
A raccoon washed up on the beach,
slowly becoming just bones.
The things your brain shows you
when it thinks its days are numbered.

I listened to the beat of his heart,
made it part of my own.
And then there's you.

My eyes started blinking
the moment I saw the light in yours.
And my hand pressed
against your shoulder in the night,
trying to ward off the nightmares.
And the fear,
almost as good as the shots in the dark
I used to take—
sticky fire through my bloodstream.
That's right—
there are three of you still in here.
My body, my brain, my pulsing heart—
none are just mine now.

My bones are all that's left of the original,
and here I am lying on the beach,
the waves taking the rest of us away,
leaving just the sun-whitened shards
of what used to hold me up.

Housemates

I have this memory—
almost a dream, but not quite—
drinking gin and Dr. Pepper,
watching a movie with you
in late spring,
in the living room,
our living room...
It had Elijah Wood and there was no one
else around to watch with us.
No one else I think
has even seen that film in the whole world.
I'm not confident
it exists, that maybe it's just
a misremembered ninety minutes.

I do know, though,
that I felt safe.
Even with the summer lurking
outside our drawn windows.
Not quite hot yet this far north,
but getting there.
And with the change of seasons
and the ebbing tides, one thing was clear—
you were my anchor
and without you, I'd drift far
past the horizon, gone away.

Remember when you lived just thirty steps down the hall?
Those were the days, man.
You lost your key; I'd lost

my boyfriend. We were so alone and so nineteen.
And without you, I'd nearly fade to nothing.
We'd graduate and I'd
become a ghost,
floating over moors, howling
out your name or maybe
just the words *best friend* in some ancient tongue
I don't even speak.

With the heat of summer
you left for the other coast,
and I vanished in a puff of smoke
to haunt you later on, but
only every other weekend.

I looked it up.
The movie was called *Try Seventeen*
or maybe *All I Want*,
depending on what year it is.
All I had left after you was the gin
and the Dr. Pepper.

I still dream we're there in your dorm room,
the bottles up above your closet
where we stashed them,
peppermint schnapps and
cherry cordial your brother bought us.
Syrup sweet down and then back up again.

When I wake, I think of you and feel an ache.
What really, though, did I lose when I lost you?
Nothing big, like a limb

or my tongue.
Maybe just a single vein
in my wrist. The one your fingers brushed
as you reached for me,
our breath sailing towards the moon,
my feet slipping over ice.
You steadied me.

And what could I have been
if I lived on your mountain—
solid ground and always a calming hand
to right me?
What could I have been?

That's in the past, forgotten
along with that movie,
a tree tumbling alone
then blending into forest floor--
it never really was.

Maggie

Write about bigger things
they told me in school.
It made me better but wasn't true.

I love a gray overcast sky
until night falls and I'm scared
of the dark again, searching

for solace in the pinprick lights
the full hanging moon.
Fitting in all the right syllables

never did make me better.
My professor went to Harvard,
drank Kombucha out of a Mason Jar

all the way back in 2003,
long before these things would turn cliché.
Thank god—she hated all things trite.

Harold Bloom was her professor
at Harvard.
She told us more than once.

I think of her only briefly,
amused,
she is much, much younger—
frozen—than I am today.

I bet she is a drug addict with lots of tattoos.
I'm an alcoholic and my hair is green.
So no judgement, Maggie? I don't think that was her name.
But maybe.

I was so homesick,
and she underlined what she wanted to "keep"
from my poems.

I'll give them to you
I remember thinking.
If you can just make me you.

A writer. A professor. Harvard.
Even the mason jar
filled with suspicious liquid

and the rusty bent bicycle
you'd ride with your long muslin
skirts hitched up.

Fuck Harold Bloom,
fuck the writer I wanted to be,
fuck clapping after words to fit in
syllables.

Most of all, fuck the rack of PBR
that sat on my dorm room floor
all semester long.

And that I drank until I fell
over and over again,
twisting ankle, bruising skin.

I bet you know all about that, Maggie.
I bet we both have been bruised by now,
skin wrinkled.
No longer ripe and ready.

Morphine

Of course the nurse would never
admit,
away from
the moldy, fluorescent reality
of the hospital
that they gave us drugs
to get us high and happy,
to make us sleep—
our fingers less itchy for their call button.
But we all knew the truth.
Are you sure your pain isn't at an 8?
she asked, preparing the syringe with
that confident flicking of a finger.
My addict brain rampaging, unchecked—
I'll say whatever number you want
if you'll give me enough of that
to replace every blood cell,
so it's not me in this bed anymore.
And I would close my eyes
and feel it in my teeth, the world
shift slightly for the better
or worse,
depending on where in the room you are
and whose eyes you're looking through.

My second time in inpatient,
someone with a clipboard was told
to take me to the nutritionist my first day.
What a mistake.
Step up on the scale

those words like a curse uttered from
the evil queen's pursed lips.
Too drunk to see the numbers
or even balance,
I fell off the scale.
Laughing from the floor, my best weigh-in yet.
How are your cravings? the clipboards
would ask weeks later, arms folded across their desk.
Oh not bad, just, you know.
When there's a vodka commercial on, then...
Not a lie.
Here we are, locked in
and in our protective circles
of steel chairs,
we ward off demons
with the sacred geometry of tangled,
repeating confessions.

But I can see mine, red-eyed still,
lurking on the other side of the fence.
Snakes for hair, waving and spitting venom.
Lying in wait for when I walk through the double doors,
maybe not that day or the next,
maybe eight years later like the furious man
in the nurse's station howled he used to have.
Too bad, your eight years hold no currency here anymore.
You're back to something single-digit,
muttering the lord's prayer
each morning with the rest of us.

Maybe this time, though—
a salt circle,
an incantation,
a book whose middle pages
have been burnt out
at midnight—
the charms will work.

I roll over at 3am still some nights,
on the worst nights,
and see the nurse's
syringe poised above my
tied-off arm
and I wait to feel it in my teeth.

Star Stickers

Tonight I feel someone else's heartbeat
in my own ear.
I'm not quick on my feet
like you,
like any of you.

On the floor in the shower I couldn't stop
from expelling it all out.
It's poison after all;
they never hesitate to remind us.
But now my body knows it
if my brain won't.

I lie with both hands out,
fingers spread wide—
crucify me.

It's so nice to have no defenses,
to leave yourself wide open.

At least then you know the attack
is always coming.

Sometimes all you have left in the world
is cold tile patterns pressing on your cheek
and the sun slowly setting
outside your small, high-up
shampoo-bottle-lined window.

I can't throw any kind of bottles out,
apparently;
soap or booze,
it doesn't matter.

But as long as I'm still here,
I'll keep cleaning up.

After all, I'm not
throwing up in a shopping bag on the highway,
but I am eighteen again in more ways than one.

Can we get some glowing star stickers
to cover our ceiling?
Like I did when I was young and
none of this had happened yet.

Hurricane Season

There is a mannequin in the neighbor's yard,
gray-shawled, grasping at an invisible loved one
but embracing only the damp, hot February air—
or maybe just making a gesture, arms half-raised, mid-pirouette.
And when I swig the Diet Coke,
I miss that sting of gin
tingling like a phantom limb in the back of my throat.
A hand I reach for, but fingers slip through.
Road Closed—Local Traffic Only.
It's been this way since hurricane season
when a man clutched his heart and moaned
I never thought it could happen here.
If not here, then where?

I'll take the mannequin's plastic hand
and we'll head down the road, into the pit
the hurricane washed into existence.
If I go out, I used to think,
I'll go out wasted;
now I'm not so sure.
I watched the waters rise,
neck craned over the side of the ark.

Wash it all away, I bray.

I always knew I was the donkey in this story.

Lunacy

You want me to walk with you tonight
and look at the full moon.
I can't, I'm sorry.
With the clouds hazy gray
it's just too much for me.
I want to look at ugly things:
tan phone receivers,
knotted shoelaces,
the disapproval in the corner of my own eye.

And I've been thinking of liquor all day
despite myself.
I read in the cards I'm working too hard.
Clinging to tradition too tightly.
Find a new way
they told me. Your footfalls behind me
made me scream.
I'm still waiting for the ambush.

Alcohol is a gorilla; you can't fucking fight it
a man in one of the squares on my screen said.
We all agreed.
We drank in cars, in closets, in jail,
bunk beds in rehab rooms stacked
like timber. *You just can't open the door
and let him in.*

Make money off us, off our agony.
I made a list of requests;
most just said, "Please be nice."
When I hear a plane overhead I brace for impact,
but I've never been in any war.

Still, shrapnel can fly in the every day.
It's when it's beautiful that's hardest.
A cool, sunny day; green leaves dripping golden;
a light rain misting over a loch
that featured in my lullabies;
or the moon like it is tonight,
gray-green cloud cover,
full to the brim and making me lose my mind.

Move In Day

In my dreams, the dorms are locked and we're moving in and out
    at the same time.
I'm searching for my car in a parking lot
and thinking that there's gin in the cupboard above the closet.

And in my dream, I forget you're married until I don't,
and then I think it should have hurt to say
your wife's wedding dress
was my favorite I had ever seen.

But really what hurts is how she went nine months in a blink of
    an eye without
thinking of a drink.
Makes me want to take a shot right now,
and if I'm admitting things in this poem, on this page,
dear reader—of course they married,
but I had no part in any of it,
unless you count all those dreams of you.

The horizon and me,
we have a lengthy history.
The waves today were choppy
and swimming towards you was hard.
You only get there, I think,
when you're not trying.

Operating Theater

I can't look at the mess
I've made of this.
Just like I close my eyes
in a movie theater while
they amputate the leg,
cut into the brain,
or pull the baby out—
wailing, always wailing.

It's not the blood.
It's not the needles.
I was never scared of either.
It's the way the knife cuts through flesh:
casual, paper-thin.
I can't stand watching
it all come apart
when it should fit together.

Sew that leg back on, Dr. McDreamy,
right after the commercial break.
Take the drill out of that skull
and most of all, put the baby back.
She doesn't want to see the light of day,
she doesn't want to be here.

Didn't anyone ask her?
There must have been a knock
at my front door,
but I didn't answer.
Hid in the living room, lights off,
I missed the message.

Where I go in my dreams
is into the hospital,
suddenly nine months pregnant—
wailing, always wailing.

You can't say no to all this, my dear daughter,
but I can.
Your screams will never hit the air, sharp and clear.
I'll hear them only in my dreams.
Or is that the church bells
calling me to my own gravestone?

Recovery

Nature abhors a vacuum
and poets a cliché,
but sometimes they creep in,
like my best dreams
are the ones where I'm someone—else—
where I drink pinky-up
in foreign countries
and jump out of planes.
Sometimes the chute opens;
sometimes it doesn't.
You're always married
and I'm always apologetic
that I couldn't keep our promises,
and when I wake now, at least I don't have to peel my dried eyelids
    off the ceiling
and labor underneath the chisel
chipping at my sanity as I vomit.

We talk about that part in meetings:
the puking that creeps up on you,
the hiding in closets,
under floorboards'
secret panels...
A pathetic sort of *Nancy Drew* mystery
where the secret in the clock
is just a bottle,
both boring and sad,
yet captivating nonetheless.

I dream also
that I'm riding on horseback
and reading Sylvia Plath in a sterile classroom.

Where is health?
I have not found it yet, my dear,
but I think I'm bringing the boat
into shore.

Lighthouse Keeper

I'm on anti-depressants,
anti-cravings, anti-anxiety,
anti-psychotics.
I am anti-it-all, pro-nothing.
I swell on the pills like a tick,
the chemicals replacing the booze
I used to pour down my gullet.
All you ever asked of me,
and still there's no satisfying you.
Peel a dead starfish off the sand;
throw it out to sea and make a wish.

How many storms did I sit here, waiting for your ship's light?
I wrote you poems and stories
you didn't like. And how many midnights did I rise alone, climbing
    metaphorical
winding stairways, creaking salty
rot sweet and stinging, to light a candle up on top, to light your way?

Lost at sea? Maybe. Or maybe just lost to me.

Is it a poor captain who blames the lightkeeper, when he crashes
    his ship onto rocks?

Lost souls one by one, tripping down the plank.

There I go.

Beach Day

I swim out,
curl into a fat, floating tick of a ball and stare
at the horizon.
I close my eyes and ask God:
Please just surround me with
open empty sea forever.

I float for a while.
The sun is there, the sky, the water,
but in the background, kids are still shrieking
and I turn and see you on shore alone,
flinching.

Inheritance

I try to explain again and again
that tipping over a sailboat
feels a lot like falling off a horse.

I don't think anyone believes me,
and I never sound more spoiled
than when I'm talking about horses
and sailboats.

The sailboats came into my life accidentally,
though maybe you could say they were in my blood
or my head, in the sea shanties
my grandmother left there. She was a sailor.
I am not a sailor. I am a barnacle clinging to your bow

and horses are in my blood.
Though no one put them there—
they were just there with the waves one day,
necks arched and falling on my shores.

It was an assault I lost in blood
and sawdust in my cheeks,
and now with the lake, the sky, the cravings,
the summer Florida storms that never
leave us alone,
I watch the world start to slip a little sideways
and I go to kick off my stirrups. And leap.
Otherwise, that horse will drag you
until you die.

It's common sense on boats or—horses—
jump off before they take you under.

I lied; I'm not a barnacle.
I *am* the horse. The boat.
And I am going down.

A circle

bound around a finger
like a promise,
they say things like it represents
endless love or that life is
a circle; it all comes back around,
at least until it stops.
Anyway,
I've seen vows taken in front of water,
under trees, by tall, grand columns.
I helped write some of them,
though they weren't my own.
Just so, I made sure all the words fell just so
off the tongue.
Just so, my kind of science
explaining the world with fantasies
and fairytales.

Don't talk at me
on a microscopic level.
The hero leaves on a quest;
he'll come back with a grail
and a bride. Then they'll trade vows
beneath a willow tree.

There have been no vows for me.
Just so, maybe I suppose the whispered ones
at midnight on an empty soccer field,
but I was the only one
who believed them in the end.

Just so,
there's no circle on my finger
to bind us and come back around,
and I fall asleep knowing
you'll leave someday, forever.

And here I am,
waiting on a leopard to change his spots
while I sit lost in the jungle,
the trees dripping on the crown
of my head, vows reciting
on repeat but never released into the air
to hover among the stamping butterflies.
My ripples stop expanding
where you stand.

Summa Cum Laude

After I graduated high school
I cried, though I didn't know why.
He held me on his lap; I was wearing
my mother's light blue dress.
All mine were black
and would have shown through
our cap and gowns all white and shiny.
I hated them.

It was the last borrowed blue white
moment I would have.

I didn't know that then.
My head pressed to his chest
while his heartbeat rose and fell
with the waves of my tears.

I was never more alone
and never closer. And I thought
This is what love is at last.

I still cry and don't know why,
but funny how my days
are shorter than ever.
Now I'm finally
almost happy,
now I've stopped
washing away the hours
in surreptitious sips
that slid into tidal waves.

What is love at last?
My dog's smile next to a yellow flower.
Your quick grin,
so fleeting and rare
but with a comet's brilliance.

I dream again and again of elevators

I'm back in the office,
a glass of red wine in hand
from some business event.
I wait a long time and it arrives with a ding.
This is the literary device
they call foreshadowing,
The doors grate open and
in I go.
It shoots up higher
than the building has floors
before it starts to plummet.
Sometimes I'm alone;
sometimes you're there
or a random work girl—I can't see her face,
just blond hair,
a collared shirt.

Sometimes I stop us
by pressing buttons
in just the right order.
They're always lettered
instead of numbers,
but the alphabet is alien.

Sometimes I don't save us
and the dream goes black, and when I wake
my feet are aching.

But sometimes I realize I'm dreaming
and I slow time down.
I spell out one last message
to you with the buttons,
then let the elevator drop again.
Can you guess what I write
in my dreams,
in the falling elevator,
over and over
until it lands
soft like it's under a spell?

And when I get out, I find you waiting.

Weather Report

The air, humid as it was, felt like a drink
with ice.
I only want what I'm not allowed
when I'm not allowed it.
If you said I could,
I'm not even sure I would.

We both know that's a lie this afternoon.
The wind kicking up like we're in Kansas or Oz,
but not for long.
Sweat and sighs and fighting matches
over counter space,
and un-harpooned, my uterus
finally releases
all that useless lifeless matter.
I bleed like a stuck pig.

When it's so still, even the sweat stops
running down my face.
I feel that I can't breathe
and then that excitement building building,
the clouds are darkening,
getting thicker.
Nothing can get me like a nice, strong pour.

Fox Hunting

It's coming like a storm in my dream,
a barn and a flea market,
a horse with colic. Rush to stop him roll
hooves kicking up in the air.

A bar always opening, always free,
liquor lined up and catching the light
as though it was sunbeams,
as though it was comfort.

I have to accept things change.
I have to see they're different now.
They say a cucumber can't turn
back into a cucumber once it's a pickle,
but then it's not a cucumber, is it?

Sobriety is full of paradoxes
and conundrums.
You have to make your own choices
but remember your brain is broken
and you are actually incapable
of making any of your own choices,
still make them for yourself
or it won't stick,
but you're re-wired now
where you can't decide.
Remember: you did this to yourself.

I never took an LSAT prep course
but this feels like a joke combined
with logic puzzle.
They tell me I should have been a lawyer.

They tell me lots of things.

Don't you get it? The liquor
hardened my heart so
I could survive, kept the fear
at bay like hounds held off
by a deep ravine,
paws scrabbling for purchase,
teeth flashing in moonlight.

Without it now, I feel that I am always
teetering at 5000 feet.
Always about to cry.
If only I could tunnel back through time
and get myself a drink.
I wouldn't care about you sitting alone in the dark,
thinking about suicide,
and me here, staring at the ceiling light
until it's too brilliant to see
and everything else is lost in the glare.

I used to always do one last shot
to seal the daylight in
where the darkness could not get to it.
Now it's all so bright it went back to black.
Did I die at 34 and this is all some joke or dream?

Don't leave me.

I wake panicked that I'm drunk,
breathe heavy in disappointment that I'm sober.
You always ask first what things cost,
but you mean the money part, not the important
things you might lose.

I smoked cigarettes in college.
It was a thrill to buy them.
Opening the pack was the best part,
like a first drink of the day,
but they only ever tasted of ash
and made me cough.
They weren't for me.

The horse standing in the field in my dream
is coated in mud and I'm
supposed to jump him five feet suddenly, though I try to explain
I barely could do three even in my best
days. Salad days. The horse eats a carrot
in my dream; his lips are soft.
I'm trying to tighten the girth,
find a curry comb,
hammer his shoes back on,
but I am no farrier—
not for me.

And a tornado sweeps through the field
in a slow slumber panic I chase after. What can be done here?
Please put my feet back on the ground.
But it's too late, I'm tossed
into another world.
The horse missed the witch and still alive,
she turned him into a vermin.
And here I am without a mount,
staring the witch down
and hearing the chittering grow fainter
as something moves away from me in the underbrush.

Impact Crater

I've got to take my pills,
stop my brain from doing
what I programmed it to do,
to survive each day in and out—
gray walls, bruised shins, broken foot.
I tripped and slurred all over the world.

But now it's changed.
Time to grow up
says a man, late forties, in our morning meeting.
I took both dogs for a walk.
It's too hot, come in soaked with sweat at 10pm.
There's never any break.
I'm still in love with everyone I've ever been in love with.
It doesn't seem to go away.
And I can't see the messes I make
until it's much, much too late.
I never claimed to be anything but sloppy
drunk and haphazard in my hours.
It's when the seconds start to beat in my skull in time with my
    panic I know I'm in trouble.
And stop asking why I can't come to you for help.
You should know it by now.
Wisdom teeth freshly yanked,
four bloody holes, and I'm seventeen again.
A date scheduled that I kept, even on Percocet
I fell in love in a Chili's.
I got up from the dentist chair,
shoved the nurse aside,
saying *I can stand up myself,*

and fell on my bleeding face,
facedown on the exam room laminate.
Help doesn't ever really help.
I knew it then, heavily medicated.
I know it now, sober,
smothered in the humid air,
the moon unclear and fuzzy.
I walk farther than I usually do
to stay out of the house a little longer.
There's a spot where kids discard their empty bottles.
I always pause as if in deference.
I keep dreaming of weddings—
never my own.

I am often a creature,
but never more than when the moon is full.

Asylum

Every night I'm eighteen again
and in my dreams I have everything
I had back then.
Everything I wanted, like

I lost my virginity right when I plotted,
seventeen just like the song.
(Though I should have just bought the condoms myself.
You were so scared outside that Circle K.)

And I haven't looked at the photo albums
in a long time,
but I don't need to. I see the pictures
so clearly every night.

My dreams betray me
and won't let me look away.

When music plays
I'm not supposed to listen to the words,
only the melody of the song, the instruments,
the pitch and key. Measure the notes
scientifically.

But I'm tone-deaf.

You still go to church,
believe in God.
I hated hymns, so suffocating
with their single mindedness.

I don't know what I believe in.
Maybe spells and full moons,
steaming cauldrons,
curses I inherited and then kept
for how I treated you.

Now look out at the hill.
Hear my cackle on the wind.
Do you think of me like I think of you,
rivers flowing parallel
from the same clear spring?
How did mine get so murky?

You're lodged in my brain like an ice pick.
I was born in the wrong time.
Earlier and I could have been lobotomized
and be rocking on a shady porch,
drool pooling at the corner of my lips.
And we both could sleep easy,
knowing I've been erased.

LARP

Last night I dreamed of a boy
I never quite loved.
I knew him for only a handful of years.
We studied for an intro to philosophy class
together in a campus café.

He played a game once a month
where he pretended to be a vampire.
So what?
We all wear masks all the time.
Why not put on a real one with a cape?

In the dream I'm dimly aware
he has a wife and kid now.
At the same time he doesn't,
and we're back in a wet, green quad—
it's spring!

It could have been me instead of her,
with a family, with a life.
But I played my cards wrong, I guess.
I lost my number.
Can I have yours?
he says with a smirk.

But I never quite loved him,
even in my dreams.
And now I'm not sure the color of his eyes,
but I think they were green. Green-
eyed boys are my weakness. Dark hair,

green eyes,
vampire fangs.
My bike lock was your birthday for the longest time.
I wanted to love him,
to blast out of your orbit,
but gravity doesn't bend
to anyone's whim,
certainly not mine. And he fell in love
with someone else:
blue eyes, blond hair.
We both fell into bed.

Now I fall asleep instead of passing out.
When the sun comes through the trees, I forget where I am.
I want a drink in the dawn more than ever
to forget who I am
and what I've left behind,
to fit the mask back on tight
and refuse to take it off again.

Don't take a sip

of my drink cause
neither of us wants to know.
Unless there's sweat on your brow
according to you
you're not really working.
Tell me if that's a joke.
I blink and it's all gone.
I'm looking at a gray sky,
catching smoky flashes
of carnival lights.
Would you ever dare?
I'm laughing at you sometimes.
You are, at me,
sometimes.
You're not really working
unless you're shoveling
a certain amount of dirt.
You glance sideways at me
more than once.
I'm pouring,
emptying
my heart out.
Is that the end?
Is that nothing?
Who knows what we know?

Meeting

Used to sit in circles
chanting;
now we stare at screens.

I'm legally blind
and I don't see well,
just want to put that out there.

It's tough.
I live alone with my ninety-pound pit bull—
he's my best friend.
What is life like without alcohol
or methamphetamines?
Treatment was good, but it gets repetitive
like life.
One day at a time, am I right?

There have been some good days,
there have been some hard days.
I get triggered when things are tough,
not like at commercials.
And things are tough a lot,
especially since my wife left me
and I can't see my kids anymore.

But I won't drink, you know,
can't take that first sip,
though there's no one here
to see me do it. No one here at all,
except my pit bull
and he doesn't mind, you know?

I know I'll die with my disease.
I just don't want to die *from* it.
And I'm just sitting here all day,
nothing to think about but what life
is like without it. Without no one.

Still.
One Day At a Time. So.

Section III

—

Screaming in my Day Dreams

Hospital

IVs dripping and tubes down throats,
suddenly back to counting seconds.
You can ask for pain relief—
make sure to be teary-eyed, but never beg.

It seems the moments of eye-closed relief get smaller and smaller
before
the countdown begins again.

Do you have kids?
Why can't I be angry at you for asking me that, stranger?
How soon is too soon to hit the call button?

Needle pushes into IV.
I feel it in my jaw, then around my teeth.
Thank god I never got into this on the outside.

The best part is the dreamless sleep. To have no cast of characters
    lurking
behind my own rhythmic breathing or under my eyelids. Not me
and certainly
not any of YOU.

Gruesome

The waking from surgery
is what being born is like.
You were existing somewhere before,
though that's behind you now
forever, and you're literally
ripped into bright light, people shouting,
and you become aware enough to know
you cannot breathe or scream or talk.

A dark-eyed woman peers over
into my field of vision,
telling me I am okay. She pulls a tube
from my throat and I choke
then choke again.

You're all right now, you're back, you made it.

I gag on the tastes mixing in the bile of my throat.
Relief, disappointment, but most of all,
horror.

I choke again.

Abyssal

On the whiteboard,
someone wrote the famous quote about the abyss
and how it eventually starts to stare back
the longer you stare at it,
but they attributed it to Mark Twain.
I don't know if it was because of
or despite the years of therapy that I paused
and corrected it. Twain would never.

Some looked confused, some annoyed. I'd prefer Mark's
dark pit to Friedrich's, I think.
I did it for me, though. And maybe a little for
Samuel Clemens,
laughing softly in his grave and the words I read in German,
a passage I underlined.
This famous quote is not even my favorite part.

Nietzsche I wrote in big red letters
underneath *abyss*
while eyes followed me around the room
back to my seat. I signed my own name
on the roster, and as I do sometimes,
came back to Kierkegaard's leap of faith.
There's an absence of faith
in this sparse room, the AC running overtime,
tattooed ankles flicking with unease around the circle
as the counselor comes in,
smirks at the board,
and then starts.

Nature

Some people are pet snakes;
not dogs
or bunny rabbits.

In case of disaster,
it's true,
rabbits will let you die
and after a while the dog might eat you
under certain dire circumstances,
but a snake will stretch
and in utter delight,
coil slowly around
again and again
until the last of your breath
lets out in a low
hisssssssssssssss.

Arachne

They went into my stomach with four small holes
and a metal spider clattering
across my rib cage.

I have not been whole now
for a very long time.
I've been treading through my dreams,
collecting pieces like I'm on a quest,
but once assembled, I fall apart
and scatter again.
Driving at night on the beach here,
eating dinner with your family, your cute-
eyed smiling kids haunting
my conversation.
Hiking in the mountains of Scotland
where I put my toes in a Loch
and there's something stirring in the dark waters
or maybe I'm just
dissolving into the night sky.
I'll wink at you and you'll see it
thousands of years later,
but for now it's
metal spider disappearing,
burrowing into gut and bone,
leaving behind empty space
where my insides once were.

Spring Training

Florida has the speed
because of the sugarcane fields down south.
They set fire to them, you know,
and chase the rabbits.
Who is fleeing, really, and from where?
Whose fate is worse: a quick end,
or a lost mind after repeated blows?
After all, the rabbits won't remember.

The flames that dance
in their black button eyes
will be forgotten soon enough.
The twitching noses will lose
the smell of smoke.
The burnt fields will recede behind them
and they'll find shelter just a little farther off,
a swampy cradle of underbrush
waiting to be a home.

No.
It's the heaving, grasping men
who you should feel sorry for.
Their futures are already in ashes,
the hits poised to land
one after another.

Until maybe one day they'll
land here, their own underbrush, sitting
in a cold room of sympathetic eyes,
urging them
to let everything go
and cry for the rabbits at last.

Turtle Soup

Are these crocodile tears?
I don't know anymore—
we're all crying together.
I wish the room was filling up,
that currents were growing stronger
and croquet flamingos flap flap
their wings while walrus tusks
grow into our mouths.
You should have been read stories at night.
Even scary ones
would have been better.
Cats that turned into red-eyed rats,
dead wives propped up with
cabbages for heads.
You should have had
fairy wings and wishes granted,
or even funny little men
in curly-toed shoes
with stupid names
howling after your firstborn
might have improved the situation.

But instead here we are,
tides of tears rising,
flotsam and jetsam
dislodge from all our saddest moments,
swirling.
But sometimes the waters
need to surge, I guess,
to wash you through the keyhole

out the other side to the beach
where a bonfire has been lit,
the pages of our pasts held close,
just starting to curl in the heat.

Potted

I've been yanking at my roots
my whole life.
I was ready to leave at sixteen
until I fell in love.
I was repotted.
I rooted deeper than ever,
not even realizing.
Was it your fault the soil was no good?

But now I'm withering.
I've been crumbling,
showing sickness with flaking bark
and dead dropping leaves
all over the backyard,
too many leaves and the grass won't grow.

And what do I do now?
My limbs all twisted up
and tied deep to the Earth,
even grasping to shift the center,
to move the poles and spiral
the whole planet out of orbit.

I can move the Earth,
but not myself
not us.

I want to rush through the other side
into stardust and the dark space
between the beginnings

and the endings of the galaxy.
I want to grow past the dirt, the worms,
the empty bottle litter
and reach through space to sunshine.

Self-Reflection

I like to leave the light on.
A grown-up way
of saying I'm scared of the dark
and what might emerge
when my mind quiets down.

It helps my anxiety
to have the TV chatter,
and when it rains I don't want
to listen too hard to the drops
on the pavement
or wind against the glass,
for fear of what I might hear.

And most terrifying
is the silver smooth surface
above my sink.
I don't dare look up
to see the lady break through
the rippling top of the lake
and press into my hands
an entire kingdom
on a sword's edge,
splitting.

No Swimming for Eight Weeks

Use *I* statements—
but don't be selfish.
Take ownership but—
admit you're powerless.

The pool is filling to the brim,
a cold glass conundrum.
We're sweating in the heat
after the rain stops,
the humidity rears its ugly head,
snorting breath from flared,
bright pink nostrils.

I dreamt of a jet-black stallion
and named him Jupiter.
He disappeared into cloud
as I got older.

I wish I'd been struck by lightning,
not thrown but maybe just dropped
from the thunder god's heavy hands.
His head is aching and he raises his palm to brow,
feeling the daughter
chiseling through his brain.

Anyhow, ash now,
I float on the breeze
into chlorinated peace
of bright blue waters

and Athena reborn
bursts from God's head at last
and declares herself cured.

She's
We're
not. But the owl on our shoulder
flaps his wings
before launching into the wind
and I murmur goodbye,
admitting

there is no thinking
my way out of this incarnation.

Black Market

The windows are tinted so it looks
to be always storming outside.
I keep having nightmares
where ghosts dangle their toes
in the pool, in the rain,

where a horse is saddled up
and waiting, but I cannot swing astride
any longer. And I wake with
a pain like a knife slicing into my stomach.

I asked for a pill to make me lose weight,
lied and said it was for depression.
The boy who jumped the fence and ran
had eyes full of ocean and a head
as empty as cathedral air.

He's gone like my dreams this morning
as I pour salt onto powdered eggs
and swig water from a crinkled bottle,
wiping my mouth after, as if it were gin.

I don't want to taste it anymore.
Just keep making incisions,
taking my organs,
and I'll keep dreaming
until the morning comes when I stop.

Genesis 11

Snakes are snakes
and people are people.
Speak up for yourself, but what if it all comes out in tongues?
We've been piling stones
on this tower of Babel
for more than a decade.

My better angels
always took the form
of glasses filled with gin.

We know the answers
Tim says to me, grim,
at the breakfast table.

He doesn't want to get married either.
You think if you hang a sign,
you can still let whoever you want walk on in,
and keep the room the same
tower straight and standing.

I smoked in bed, sorry.
Threw the mattress out the window.
Flaming, it fell from the sky,
trailing feathers like cast out angels.

Where will you sleep with me gone?
And more importantly,
when your hubris brings the tower down,
who will lift you from the rubble,

examine your split tongue,
and determine to teach you
human speech again?

Check the Single Box

Who has a family?
I did not raise my hand.
You would be mad.
Say it's all self-pity.
And that we are indeed family,
though you won't make any promises.

I have no husband.
Have no kids.

I did not raise my hand.

And why aren't you enough?
And you won't make any promises.

But you never said you would.
I never said I'd put down.
Find a life where it was unnecessary
and no longer made up
all of my bones.

What kind of rings
would carbon dating find around my throat?
At night, the ugly scar there grins
and leaks liquor.

I didn't raise my hand.
My family was always sloshing
behind glass
and then running right through me.

Raise your hand
you'd say.
Snap out of it
you'd say.
Don't lie
you'd say.

Cross my heart,
hope to die.

I'm telling our secrets
after all this time.
I can say at least
those are mine too.

Same Sands

You two were in the same desert
at the same times
but never saw each other,
though brain matter
must all look the same
as you're cleaning it from truck seats.

And whether either of you
should have been there
is not for me to say
(though I have said it).
Who's to say?
Whose it is, really?
But that's not the point
here in this room.
It's beside the point,
really.
The point is your wife
called you a liar and took the kids
and now there are track marks
all up your shins.

I never had to scrub
a friend's scattered mind
out of seat cushions,
and certainly I can't say
of all things
that I am a bad father.

But we both drank
until we were blind,
and we still can't see all that well.
People in our lives
have left us behind,
and we still have not caught up.

What can we do but send
well wishes out in bottles,
and struggle together
in the same hot sun?

White People Shit

is what they call asking for help,
airing our problems out,
fancy linens on the line.

Maybe it's not right,
but I am thinking
we are closer than we realize.

Recalling the long line
of Presbyterian ministers
on my one side, who surely never encouraged
anything but a pristine white
clapboard exterior. Casserole dishes
scoured clean after Sunday potlucks.

And the other side, Jackson.
Didn't I, even in the midst of this white
people shit, clench my jaw and just say
Well, he was poor and adopted from Alabama.

Someone's lying there the girl said. I'm honestly
not sure what she means. They *were* poor
and he ran away to Canada
and fought in Korea and then came home to beat
his wife and kids senseless and took long pulls
of whiskey in his morning glasses of milk and he busted
up my uncle's kidneys and no one
did anything or said anything and my uncle died
when I was fourteen and I didn't know why until much later.

I'm sure there are lots of people lying.
I'm sure not saying any of this now out loud.
White people shit,
and all I know is I haven't been near
Africa since I was primordial ooze.
I don't know
what I don't even know.

But I guess
in the northern most islands of Scotland,
Vikings frequently visited
to express themselves.
White people shit
at its purest.
Setting fire to villages,
screaming wet wood aflame,
screaming bloody people,
watching the clashing red-orange flames
mingle together
with ethereal green-blue aurora lights.

Far enough North, my bones feel satisfied.
Snow is packed into my blood.
Hot and cold.
Fire red, ice blue.
The world snaps its jaws around its own tail.
We keep circling in the sea of stars.

Bacchus

I'm clenching my jaw,
trying to remember
the god of wine's Roman name.
Not the Greek!
It clicks quickly.
I feel like an alien,
the back of everyone's eyes
drilling into me and rushing
to my head like wine.

Pour it down my throat;
the only thing here
is cranberry juice.

I have it with my eggs
every morning.
The color red looks good on you.

My insides feel
like they've been poured
into a mixing bowl.

I feel like an alien.

I want to run my fingers
through the stars,
let them slip through
to fill my goblet
before it reaches my lips.

Ghosts

You can say you're so glad
you were never good at all that
book shit,
and yet you
speak in verse without knowing
the consequences. I'm trying
to explain theater of the absurd.

Once, I read a book where aliens invaded
simply to tell all smart white men
they needed many wives
and many children,
and then they would transcend
into infinite beams of white light.

I laughed out loud at the ending.

My friend says she's afraid of the dark.
I mumble *Me too.*
Without him next to me,
I'm always leaving a light on.

The sun is painting our old motel pink.
Is three the magic number?
We're all superstitious here.
We don't step on cracks.
We don't count on good luck.
In nine days, I'll catch a ride home.
I'm living in single digits now,
seeing new faces emerge,
old ones disappear into a dream.

Here is my promise
and my absurdity.
I'll remember.
I'll remember you all.

Step One: Powerless

My brothers send me pictures of their children
as though now that they've
procreated, all is forgiven.

How loud can I scream
but still be silent?

I write snide notes
about God and his twelve steps
in my margins. I am margins.

Behind the scenes, who's funding
the stale coffee and do their
reptilian eyes roll
in different directions
so they can see all the sinners?
Sure, it's not ALL church basements,
particularly not in Florida—
we'd be up to our necks
in swamp water, after all.

Dammit,
I don't want to think
about any of this anymore,
but we don't have that luxury,
do we?

Unless of course I go back,
look at the pictures,
the mirror smiles from my childhood

slipping into today,
knocking bottles off the shelf,
down my throat,
sinning unoriginally.

Dammit.
Damned.
Powerless after all.

Alternative

In rehab reality
I know to wait in line for meds,
even at dawn that first week,
and I know there will be people pacing
and spitting and yelling
at the nurses and I just need
to keep my mouth shut until
it's time to open it for pills.

In the 5am nurse's station,
there's no older sister who throws
her dice across the room in frustration
when the game doesn't go her way.

In rehab reality someone asks me if I was
in the military and they're serious.
In rehab reality the nurses show me pictures
of Halloween décor on their phones
because I'm nice to them
and they think I might be a witch.

There's no partner here who can't
put away the dishes or forgets
to pick up stray dog toys.

In rehab reality I suddenly know
a lot about vaping. I give a sad crack
addict the last brownie. I know all the counselors
like we're old friends, and we kind
of are.

In rehab reality I know which groups to avoid
and which to never miss. In rehab reality someone
from the streets calls me hardcore.
In rehab reality I give medical advice I shouldn't,
and then say *But ask your doctor*
as though they might have the wherewithal to sue me later.

In rehab reality I say the words *Get a lawyer* at least once a day.

There's no one here who can't seem to keep
her room straightened out. The person who my mother-in-law
says is lazy or my brother-in-law says is useless
does not exist anymore. She has vanished into musty
motel air.

In rehab reality I draw in my notebooks and tall marines
tell me *Those are sick* then show me
their tattoos. In rehab reality I pray often
for people not to overdose,
to make it to next year.

In rehab reality the nurses tell me they can't believe
I'm walking around after major surgery.
In rehab reality they slip me extra Advil when I clutch
my side and moan. In rehab reality the boy next to me
turns and calls me kind. Then he pauses, looks again
at my eyes,
and repeats himself.

In rehab reality I sing karaoke in front of a crowd.
I share everything out loud instead
of sitting all day long with it looping

through my head and into my stomach
where it aches until I try to drown it out.
In rehab reality the BHT will let me keep illicit shampoo
after I promise I won't drink it.

No one calls me spoiled
or princess,
and one lady asks me what
"putting money on the books" is,
and I answer though I've never been to prison.
In rehab reality people ask me what I think.

In rehab reality fights break out,
the food is sometimes awful,
laundry comes out smelling the same
as it did when it went in and the first night when my gall
bladder was exploding I sat on the bathroom floor
and couldn't even cry, I just begged god to let me die
before walking to the nurse's office
and calmly asking for a ride to the ER.
In rehab reality I miss you so badly
it feels like I have a phantom limb.

In rehab reality I have no children.
In rehab reality I have no husband.

Some things are the same.

In rehab reality most of the people you meet will die.

Eventually rehab reality will end. Techs will volunteer to carry
all your things because you were so nice to them.
Then you will become the spoiled princess
who can't pick up after herself,
who can't seem to get up fast enough
when the dog steals a toilet paper roll
and then there are white streamers all over the yard,
flags of surrender, shaking hands.
And you will have to bend and buckle
under each hour of the day, and everyone
will expect the two realities
to combine into some magic elixir
that cures you.

You will find yourself six months later,
watching your nephews across a table,
one refusing to put on his pajamas. You
will find yourself suddenly furious
in the middle of losing a game,
you will fling the dice across the table.
Then you will find yourself head in hands, crying
in the bathroom and thinking
Why can't I just have a goddamn drink.

And you will hate yourself for thinking that,
and you will wish everyone could visit
the places you have been
and see the person who, standing in the hallway,
held a girl who just got the news
she wasn't getting her kids
and told her it wasn't worth
using over.

But they can't and won't,
and they will say they don't care about your poems
or even worse, not bother to read them.

And this is okay.

You have one reality
and you cannot split yourself
into so many tiny pieces for everyone else's.

Someone from four years ago rehab reality messages you
hey he says
we're still alive! we're still in recovery!
we might be the only ones left.
congrats to us.

And you'll stare a long time at this message.
And try to congratulate yourself.
But you can't.

Incoherence

I will go days and days without eating.
They taught me that in Sunday school,
only when under the holy influence.
Go out to the desert
when the spirit commands it.

I shove my tongue against my teeth.
I had so many nights to myself.
So many nights to drink until
I saw Jesus, arms outstretched
like his are supposed to be.
But I had no time for an embrace,
just wanted to know most
what he saw in that desert.

My dog is barking.
I am wishing I spoke more languages
than just the one and a half.
I used to be able to tell you in German:
This will be settled tomorrow.
I'm too drunk right now.

A gingerbread house of candy,
two nephews facing each other.
I say, *In college, we called these list poems.*
And then I took the bags of scrambled eggs
and poured them into skillets, work study
in the morning,
and when I rode my bike to my dorm
I fell sideways into the snow bank
before I could get my balance.

If I paid more attention
to what I saw in the cold air, then
maybe it could have saved me.

Healing Process

It can take four weeks
for all the inflammation to go down.
My guts have caused
me no end of trouble.
Yet you say I should trust them.

Just thinking of walking back through our door,
my stomach turns.

We have so much,
but I put my hand out for more.

Press a five into my palm.
Some days it doesn't feel very good.
The pool is hot and I can't swim anyhow.
The incisions are too fresh.
It's fun to remind people
I've lost an organ recently.

It's almost time to wait in line.
There are graves reflected in the windows
people used to leap out of,
trying to make it into the water
then leaving with broken limbs.

We breathe in and out.
They try to teach us patience.

Yet when we wait in hot hallways,
someone always ends up screaming,
storming off in disgust, kicking
the trash can over on their way out.

Ready or Not

I have not drawn the moon once
the whole time here,
a month of constant nightmares
and watching the sky turn purple
from my bed each morning.
I'm not ready for any of this.
And so what?

I don't want to end up planted nearby
with no one to visit me,
and so I have to make the changes,
swim with the current
instead of against it for once.

Section IV

—

Slouching towards Awake

Highway Driving

And how, suddenly,
have I become a mechanism
again in an instant? So quickly.

Rusted, not fitting together
the right way. You're constantly
just polishing and peering
into a stainless steel heart—
you keep mistaking it for mine.

I have been one recently
and long ago cold stethoscope
against my chest, arm hanging
limp and bloody.
I just pretend it isn't mine anymore.
Poked and prodded in the literal sense,
pricked by my toes and high arches
of my feet. I waited breath by breath
for the next shot of morphine, the
Dilaudid, anything that went into the IV
and made my eyes unfocused.
Can't you see
I don't want to see?

Your blind mechanism
with one last sad whir
shuts down.

It took forever to get to the highway this morning
and once merged I started shaking.
Humans were not meant to hurtle at these speeds
so early on a Monday morning.
The highway lines that litter
a thousand country songs flew
up and kicked at my windows.

I'll draw from a different deck today,
shuffle the new cards, breathe
in the fresh promise of the paper.

These were made in the Ukraine,
where maybe they still believe in magic.
They did in the Czech countryside—
they whispered about fairies,
told us to keep our eyes out for trolls. I hiked up
and down the rolling hills, thinking
of what and who
I had lost. Thinking of how
I could have kept him.

The traffic in Atlanta is worse than here.
But still it takes forever to get downtown.
I remember thinking maybe someday...
who knows what the future might hold,
that exact same way
I believed in fairies
and checked among ancient twisting roots
for gossamer wings.

Of course you know
none ever appeared,
and we only met once more over coffee and I pretended
it didn't feel like an asteroid impact,
a wall of ocean coming across the parking lot.

Did I shake his hand?
I can't remember. I pull into the garage.
Four years and more it's been,
in and out of treatment,
a normal addiction story:
down and up then down again.

Who knows what the future holds?
Maybe fairies hurtling
along highways,
wings flickering like headlights,
magic dust floating in the breeze,
changing the cards I draw,
rewriting the past—

illuminating the future.

Hand Out

I gave the man named James
a twenty dollar bill,
though we both knew
he wasn't going to spend it all
on a shower or food.

But who am I to possibly judge?
I have been contemplating the line
between where I sit now in my humming car
and where he stands on the hot sidewalk
for years now. Calculating odds of survival
in my head—I may not be good with numbers,
but even I can't make enough mistakes
to make my survival likely.

James skips off. I know the bounce in his step
as well as if it were my own feet dancing
down the street. I pull out the other direction.

As I merge, a crushing urge to join him
washes over me. I have to resist.
I hope he does get some food
and a shower. And if not, at least
I hope he gets some comfort
and sweet dreams. And I am just grateful
he called me beautiful.

Third Life

A drink is lifetimes away,
like the hospital room
whose wall color I've already forgotten.
It's always lurking behind the mouthwash,
the strange texts we read from friends
we can't help.

The wheel is spinning. I keep drawing swords—
that is not my suit, but yours.

I'm cups but have to be careful
to feel the exact correct amount,
measured like flour
then released in a white cloud
when mixed up too quickly.

I lay for hours, mind blank
on a tattoo table.
How could I feel at home there
but not in my own skin anywhere
else? I fell asleep while the needle
was still whirring.

To let something go
means you're making room for something new.
This state and I have too much in common.
We run hot and wear everyone down.
We don't give way to autumn but cling
to green leaves until they curl up brown
in the hot sun.

Take your damn flip flops and throw them in the bonfire
that we don't get to have because it's still 95 degrees
outside and in my guts. The flames sow discontent in my
furrowed brow as nightmares play out each evening.

I command you.
Feed your bare feet to an alligator—taking the toes
one by one.
I wake up in panic, thinking
the sun has baked out all my compassion,
and I am tough and tattooed now I say
to myself in the mirror like they told me to.
But I don't believe in any of it.
And still I wait and hope and even pray sometimes
for heavy snowfall.

Water Line

I always want the highest tides. I'm ready
for waters to rise. So sad to see the wet sand
strewn with black knotted seaweed,
the scattered shells, drained of magic,
bleached by sun. All just waiting for the waves
to wash over them again and bury them deep.

I don't want low tide walks
damp grainy sand stuck in between toes
boats jammed into beaches— oars
useless at their sides.
The ocean covers it up like fresh snow.

I prefer my landscape blanketed.

I never liked the feeling of the currents gathering strength
plotting way offshore to come rushing back,
a beach invasion every evening,
the moon growing larger and more pregnant by the hour
as it rises above the darkening crests.

There are so many words for this.
Ebbing and Flowing.
Waxing and Waning.
Coming and Going.

The fluctuations of a spinning planet.

On a soggy, empty beach once
I tried to generate my own gravity,
twirling both hands out,
fingers becoming rings like Saturn's
blurred into horizon, sea, sand.

I fell and felt the grains dig into my knees.
felt my skin scrape
and the coastline pressing like a wet washcloth
against my sweating brow.

We are spinning and the ocean
ebbs and flows,
and people enter and exit
stage right or left or from above,
suspended by guy wires.

When I close my eyes I will see all your faces,
spinning spinning spinning.

I am only at home when the waters are at their highest,
when you don't need to go too far
before you are up to your chest
then on your knees, your head
is all the way under
and breathing out all the bubbles
break onto the surface.

Someday they will be all that anyone sees of you.

No Small Parts

Recently it feels
like when I reach for words
they're used already.
Debris washed up on the shore
of a lake, not the ocean.
Everything scaled down.

I am still having these dreams
where I try to call a boy I knew
a long time ago now
and he never ever picks up the phone,
and his wife is at his elbow
anyhow. Why do I still care so much,
even if only while asleep,
whether he answers me?

I forgot that before I realized
I could not act or sing,
I thought I might want to be on stage.
I got there once at age seven, and terrified,
nearly fainted dead away
while Yankee Doodle Dandy
played at full volume behind me.
I trod the boards only for an incoherent
thirty seconds.

This morning in group
someone said something new
along with those same sayings

we all chant like monks,
each line getting more high-pitched
and shrill, a scratched CD skipping.
"The Doctor's Opinion", "12
in 12", "Amends is not an apology",
"Put it in milk."

He said, "You can't see your reflection
in boiling water." Can't you, though? I thought,
imagining staring into the pot,
nose so close the tip is burnt. Bubbles making eyes
bulge out.
The idea is a comfort.

"If someone raped someone else's daughter,
I'd shoot him," said another one.
"It would be justified." Would it?
I don't think so, but I'm not
going to start an argument. Another girl is, though.
"Are you god?" she demands. "ARE YOU?"
With her shout I feel myself
begin to shut down, shrink down
to something small and frozen.

I smile the rest of the three hours.
Answer questions.
Another man is here today
and was here with me two years ago,
and will be here into the future stretching
before us like a hall of mirrors.
We're riding this carousel into the ground.

And turns out I'm a better actor
than even I realized,
and that my stage career has persisted
like a dark, long-limbed parasite,
deep through my whole life.

At Sea

The dreams I'm having
are suddenly all on boats.
The worst are the ones
on giant cruise ships where
I end up falling into churning wake
and I wake.

And I prayed, Please
let it not be the pancreas
and I won't drink ever again.
Neither God or I
believed me for a second,
but it felt good to say for once.

You're supposed to stop making promises
at some point; you realize
it just isn't safe.

I've ruined so many paintbrushes,
left them in dirty gray water too long.
I never cared what tools I had
to do the job,
just that it was done and over with
as fast as possible.
Scotch tape, pushpins, tiny watch screwdriver.

The problem is it all falls down
in the end.

All aboard—
we're setting sail
and we might never find land again.

Birds

I am weeping feathers from my eyes,
peacock green and dull black and brown.
Golden gazes the sun is blinding.
I don't want to talk about this anymore.
Go to bed angry,
wake up in confusion.
Strong black coffee each day is so many hours,
stuck in my pupils like a splintered board.

Don't rub if there is something lodged
in there; you'll never see again.

People don't like the smell of horses.
All I want is a chance to ride.
I would love to live in a barn.

The feathers are accumulating.
If you line your nest, will I stay?

I'm crying over hatching eggs,
counting them as they emerge,
each one alive until the last.

Evolution

I want to peel my skin off.
It hangs so heavy,
filled with depression sinking
as fast as hot air rises. Like a sail
too full so it snaps and the boat
stalls.

Tonight somehow I can feel his touch
as though we were just seventeen.
I want to scrub him off of me,
but nothing ever works.

Disinfect, chug, vomit.
I don't want to go back to the beginning.

Or maybe the beginning
is where I should be.
Way before seventeen.
Invertebrate
refusing to crawl from the sea.

Shuck my flesh,
flex my exoskeleton.

We were both there, weren't we?
When time began
and when it ended too.

In Which We Enter a Bar

What will they call us years later?
My mom talks about my brother in law
once-removed
who might get engaged soon
after just a couple of years.

That's what people do,
I say,
watch her wince.

What will they gossip about besides
she should have just gotten over it?
I have been labeled a brat,
spit pooling at my toes,
and when I drink right from the bottle
the shock is ridiculous.

In this one dream
I'm sitting at a huge table
filled with people I knew only
briefly
in other lives.

I'm always waiting on you.

I'm trying to order a double gin and tonic
by blinking at the waiter in morse code.

Is there something in your eye? he asks.

Despairing, I go to the bathroom
and pocket a bottle on the way there.
A moose on the wall sees me do it,
begins to sound out a deep alarm.
I dive into the cool liquid surface of the mirror
and hear glass shatter behind me.

You're not there waiting for me.

What will they call us, though,
when we're dead and buried alongside each other?
My bones rotten, fingernails breaking down.
If I'm not even enough now,
what will I be when I am only remains?

Woman in the Dunes

Look—
one of my favorite books
takes place in sand dunes
on some Japanese sea.

The whole story is an allegory:
sand piling on sand,
an innocent man at the bottom
of an inescapable pit.
It's bleak, sure,
but don't forget there's a woman there,
cheerful
to keep him company.

He just went on a holiday
to look at some bugs
and then suddenly he's down at the bottom
of everything. The ladder
is taken away by some unseen power,
and he's stuck.

At first he fights it;
he does not want to be there.

Eventually though the woman
is expecting his child and the sand keeps piling
higher and higher
and the reader laughs
that he just wanted to study beetles
and now he can't think his way
out of this hole, away from this woman.

And isn't the point of the story
that our hero is forced to—yet shouldn't—care
when the mother lies sideways and bleeding in the end?

The reader sees,
there's a ladder propped up—
he could escape,

but she is giving birth.

What if the story turns?
It hinges
on if the man cares about the baby,
if he rushes up the ladder
for help or to get away and instead
he freezes—
he just stops in the middle of the pit
and looks up,
sand falling in his eyes.

Let me explain,
it's an existentialist fable—
the protagonist examines all his specimens,
alone,

the woman gives birth,
and the reader knows the baby died.

Spirit of Impurity

I've been summoning demons
for over a decade.
Careful,
you're still a beginner.

And I've learned to control them
until I can't.

Today I knew exactly
how Jonah felt inside that whale.
Deep angry siren
songs lodged in my ears,
panic embedded in memory
as the MRI ticked through the pictures.

You did great,
the technician said.
I didn't open my eyes once.

I have no more dignity,
nowhere to go from here
to gain any on my own.

I would shoot myself in the head,
I said once.
You didn't get it.
You don't get it.

You say we have a family.
At night we fall asleep next to each other.
No one ever left you
like they did me.

What could I have been?
Married and on a horse.
Mount up,
heels down.
If I gallop all alone,
will I get something back?

The key here is dignity.
I lost it at nineteen and swore
I never would again.
Reading in the bright green
quad, grass sunlit and feeling
finally better and over him.
I could speak several languages
and the future was cracked wide open
like I wasn't smoking Winston cigarettes.

But then I lost it all over again:
shit in a bedpan,
couldn't move my legs.
Hallucinated mermaids armed to the teeth,
vampires and otters,
bombs exploding,
and me in a metallic bikini.
Exposed exposed
exposed.

I studied Sylvia Plath,
Audre Lorde.
A girl I sat next to in class
many times
made a movie and got famous.
I pulled off the road
when I heard her name come through my speakers.

At least when there's
no more pride to salvage,
there's less work to do.
You go through all my things,
no more rights.
You've paid for it all,
after all after all.

It's all really yours anyway.

I sit in the car in the driveway,
the only thing left.
I watch you take my keys,
pocket them away.

I have nothing but ash in my tongue,
and I'll put on a show
while you dump out whatever I hid.

I frame some pictures
of us.
I hope you see them
and don't wince.

It's foolish.
In Amsterdam I was drunk,
but I admired Rembrandt,
Van Gogh. I'll trace
the past like well-worn paths
and plant my feet against
the future.

You said I'd be upset
this morning
and then you said
I don't care about anything,
as though
rewriting history
is your new business.

Dali we admired together,
but he is open
for so much interpretation.

You shout at me
across a canyon filled
of elephant swan,
of melting clocks.

I shake like a dog,
my belly hurting,
my ears still listening
for the parking lot CD
we found outside of Asheville,
scratched beyond recognition
but when the music came on,
his smile still lights up
the inside of tonight.

Swampland

Walking down the path I used to jog
once upon a time,
when these broken boardwalks were new.
I'm not even
that old,
but the humidity will do that—
break things before their time,
seep into deep wooden cracks
until everything comes apart.

I used to huff and puff
along the dirt while you
were off exploring foreign lands.
You're always expecting me
to forget the hours my tracks kept me
in line and how
you joined in and condoned and
condoned.

The just doing my job defense
didn't hold up well historically, but now

that I've brought that up
I've lost the argument again.
Naturally it happens
when you major in German history,

but that's been decades ago.
Almost

though
really
I am not that old.
And I look at the sodden boardwalk
succumbing to the swamp.
Only a Florida girl
knows to listen for an alligator's bark.

I don't trust you
like I don't trust raccoons.
No moral imperative.
Bandits
that steal your heart
and then stuff themselves
full of your garbage.
They refuse
to cough it back up—then
they complain that their stomachs hurt.

Winter is Still My Favorite Season

Why can't I stop thinking of you this time of year?
And suddenly, like lightning,
I realize
that this is when we fell in love, holding hands,
running from one gazebo
to the next
in the park
where my friends would get married
so many years later
and I just got drunk.

I paint my nails alien green.
If I had kids I wouldn't have the time.
That's worth it, right?
I hide my bottles in dirty laundry
and laugh too loud in theaters.
And everyone wants a piece
of my addiction.
I envy the man at the streetlight
until the very second I'm about to be him.

Still I wish I could cut the delicate
threads of this web.
Or at least struggle harder
until the spider comes
to put me out of my misery at last.

Shopping at Five Points
we flipped through posters.
One is still on my wall
and in my dreams
you point to it.

Going South

Always thought I'd be good with mothers.
Turns out they hate me, every one.
Or maybe I'm picking the boys
who they can't let go of.

I stopped writing this to Google your mom.
How is that helping anyone anymore?
Except I hate that she hates me.
I suspect you don't talk now.
That things went really South.

But who am I to say I told you so?
You were always in the right.
And this is turning into
a letter to you,
so let's change the subject.
I keep dreaming of the street where I went to college.

I rode my bike down the sidewalk,
not knowing that was illegal
and maybe I told you about it,
or maybe that was after.

And what is this need
to connect, to be forgiven endlessly?
We both made amends
and I reached out, even though
I knew I shouldn't.

So why in my dreams
am I still writing you?
Typing and typing,
waiting for your answer like
I'm seventeen again and it's cold outside
and I've had my wisdom teeth removed
and you're standing at my door
making puns, grinning, arms outstretched
as you open the car door for me.

I want to go back,
look at your picture,
but if I do
I think I'll turn
into a pillar of salt
and melt in the rain.

Golden Apples

Both awake and asleep yesterday,
I couldn't let anything go
and what's hard for you
is hard for me too.

What can you trust
less than a serpent's split tongue?
The snake never ate the apple,
too worried about calories
and staying slim.

Perhaps ageless and unbound
by geography it also curled, starving
around the apples of the Hesperides
draconic teeth, catching the golden light
reflected off their thin skins.

Maybe now the snake will turn,
take a big bite
then spit out the chewed up flesh.
Waiting for a hero to come and
don't doubt she'll attempt to devour him whole
while the apples chime out
metallically, unnaturally,
as mother eats son below.

Group Work

I dream fiercely and often.
I started to memorize my favorite poem
but didn't make it all the way.

I want to be both drunk and sober at once
and I hate lying.

I love lying said one man,
teeth bared.
They send you away to these places
then wait impatiently to receive you back, fixed.
All you know is you're broken
in the first place.

A man had his car stolen three times in one night
by the same woman.
Stop sleeping with prostitutes
we said.
Another wandered three states worth of highways
taking pictures of church billboards
to keep track of where he'd been.
Stop snorting coke
we said.

I talk my relationship.
He needs to put a ring on it
they say.
He doesn't value you
they say.

I know this last thing is not true in my bones.
I also know the first thing is true in my bones.

What does it say about me
that I wish I were someone else?
Throw the bones skyward,
read them where they land.
Which truth surfaces faster?

When I see the ocean,
that's when it breaks like waves.

Echidna

mother of monsters
looks innocent and beautiful
from the waist up
beneath though,
sunk into the evil earth,
she tills with wicked tail
to plant her seeds.
Her
coils and scales
writhe upon
scales and coils.

Her smile can be sweet
with her mouth closed,
but open you can see she is all fangs
and venom.

She is always
calling to her children,
but don't let them fool you
with their limps and wounds.
It is all a grand performance so
they can
still leave you for dead,
whisper angry words in your ears,
fill your insides with bubbling lava.
Betrayal is their artform.

Echidna
is only instinct
her eyes roaming
for dangers to her brood.
There is not time for reason.
She would never recognize a friend
or gentle hand extended.
Only danger is reflected in her eyes.

She deceives herself
that she could keep watch forever.

But she cannot
for she has been blinded
by gazing into
the boiling sun that is her heart.
All that heat and light—
it does not allow for comprehension.

But there are only so many enemies
and friends to take care of
before she is finally alone.
What would she see
if you placed a mirror before her?

She is no Medusa
to freeze into stone,
preserved until a new age dawns;
she does not know how to let go
or to look away.

Perhaps
her eyes would burn themselves out,
the bright hatred within burrowing
dark black holes into her pretty face.
Ash dripping from eye sockets,
she would turn to her brood for help.

When she shrieks, her monstrous children
will come to her, to feast upon her
while she smiles,
knowing she gave them life once more,
a chance to gnash at the Earth
with razor handsaw teeth,

sure as though they were pruning a fruit tree
and beneath the ground,
her lower half,
unable to rest in peace,
still twists in spite and hatred.

Singularity

Even now years and so many nights,
clear-eyed and without it,
the seeds of fear begin to grow
at sunset like night blooming flowers—
beautiful maybe, but
unsettling in their neon colors.

It used to be I would have to chug
cup fulls to sedate myself, and falling asleep
was truly falling—a law of gravity,
an inevitable darkness at the bottom
of the day's ravine.

Once when I was trying to get sober,
I snuck into my parent's kitchen and rifled
through their fridge for expired orange juice.
I just needed a little
to splash into the glass.

And then peace and no more earthquakes
for three blissful hours
until their screams and the sound
of liquid down the drain woke me.

I remember squinting at the brightness
of their morning anger in confusion.
They may as well have told a goldfish
he had to start breathing air now.

Then there'll soon be the sound of him
going down the drain.

Tonight there's nothing to pour and
it's a relief.
Still I find my breath coming faster
as bedtime approaches.

Small, I was afraid of black holes.
Spending hours fretting and tossing,
thinking of unknowable horrors,
of black oblivion
oozing towards our home planet.

I would fall fitfully asleep at last, only
to dream of hooded figures
with long silver knives leaning over my parent's bed,
me, my brothers...

Now without any sedation,
gravity does not apply
and I find myself floating in moonlight,
hand on my old dog's side,
feeling his breath rise and fall.
I am drifting rather than plummeting
easing into peace,
like a tide creeping up.

Still some nights I long for
that headlong gulping crash
into a black hole sea.

I have a confession:
deep down I admit
I believed if I swam deep enough,
I'd travel through time
and be able to start over.

Cassandra

Did I love you in fact
because you would not promise forever?

I will jump off of the highest cliffs
over and over again all alone,
but hold my hand
and I am suddenly terrified.
Dare to stand near the ledge yourself
and I will cover my eyes.

When did I first read the words
"rich interior life" and how did I know
they weren't a compliment?

Heroes mostly journey alone
and *hush* let's forget they end up
with arrows in their heels
or murdered by their evil uncles.

I do remember when I first read
"fatal flaw" and knew I didn't
have just one.

Everyone talks about Achilles,
but what about Hector?
He's the one whose broken body
really pissed off the Gods.

Again, the things you know
instinctively upon a first read.
I am not Hector
or Horatio.
I am Achilles
and Hamlet. And it's only a matter of time
before lightning smites me.

But no, not really,
I am Cassandra,
maybe with some Ophelia thrown in.
I see things so clearly but
no one believes me,
and I keep insisting love
can save me
despite all evidence against it.

And I am forever retreating
into madness.
It's the safest space for me.

And where do you fit in
to my mythology?

You're emphatically not Ajax, no,
and certainly not Paris—
you hate cities and
no one has ever said, even squinting,
that I could be Helen.
That's alright,
I find it reassuring that
no ships will ever launch
towards this face.

Still, please don't stand so close to the ocean,
I swear I saw a tentacle just off the shore
and I don't fully trust the god of the sea.
Without you, after all,
nothing is keeping me from
my arrow to the heel, my sword in the gut, my cliff's edge
death after battle after
everything has been lost—just one final insult
as the gods all laugh from above.

I told you this would happen.
I told you
rings hollow and sad when
there is no more to be done
because it is all over.

Ithaca

In the rosy-fingered dawn
I keep thinking I've forgotten something.
Not down the hall or on the coffee table
but in my sleep last night—
a set of keys swinging in the lock.

And I need to learn to let things go.
Let things go,
the gods whispered to Medusa through
her hissing curls.
Just let the grudge, the injustice fall away...
they told Medea crying over her children's
broken bodies.
Cast your golden eyes down.
Forgive yourself. Forgive them all.
Forgiveness is freedom.
Forget the rest.

Just don't turn on the light,
you cannot lay eyes on me
but sleep with me now,
Cupid said to Psyche.
It's for your own good.
She couldn't take him at face value,
just a dimmed candle and bare chest
in the dark.
Let it pass, let it go,
radically accept.

Have faith and just live laugh love,
God said to Jonah
in the belly of the whale,
shuffling his divine sandaled feet to keep
them out of fishy stomach bile.

The stories end like this:
Jonah escapes the whale.
Psyche held her lantern high.
Medea takes up poisoning.
Medusa begins turning men to stone.
And they pay prices but never
did they hoist a white flag above their castles.
And me?

I don't want to be an aimless breeze
slipping through your fingertips.

I want to be a strong north wind
snapping at your sails, pulling
them taut and taking us home.
We'll creep onto the shores
older, wiser, and in disguise.
With the help of a goddess
and her owl, we'll drive out unwanted suitors
to claim our birthright
and fall asleep beneath familiar stars
at long last.

In the morning we will wake,
and our dreams will continue
into daylight.

Acknowledgements

Thank you to all the staff and counselors at White Sands Treatment Center in beautiful downtown Plant City, Florida. You not only save our lives, but you make us feel safe and human while doing it.

About Atmosphere Press

Founded in 2015, Atmosphere Press was built on the principles of Honesty, Transparency, Professionalism, Kindness, and Making Your Book Awesome. As an ethical and author-friendly hybrid press, we stay true to that founding mission today.

If you're a reader, enter our giveaway for a free book here:

SCAN TO ENTER
BOOK GIVEAWAY

If you're a writer, submit your manuscript for consideration here:

SCAN TO SUBMIT
MANUSCRIPT

And always feel free to visit Atmosphere Press and our authors online at atmospherepress.com. See you there soon!

About the Author

CAITLIN JACKSON is a poet and has been in recovery since 2019. She is a graduate of Oberlin College and has an MFA from University of Central Florida. She has had her works published in such journals as *Painted Bride Quarterly*, *Natural Bridge*, and *Cathexis Northwest Press*. She and her longtime partner are lucky to live with the best timeless mythical being of all, their mutt Erebus, and they are very excited to be opening their own dog daycare franchise some time in this upcoming year. They reside together outside of Orlando, Florida, though Caitlin eventually hopes to move somewhere with lots of ice and snow. This is Caitlin's fourth full-length poetry collection.